SHAUN WHITE

BY ANTHONY K. HEWSON

abdopublishing.com

Published by Abdo Publishing, a division of ABDO, PO Box 398166, Minneapolis, Minnesota 55439. Copyright © 2019 by Abdo Consulting Group, Inc. International copyrights reserved in all countries. No part of this book may be reproduced in any form without written permission from the publisher. SportsZone™ is a trademark and logo of Abdo Publishing.

Printed in the United States of America, North Mankato, Minnesota
042018
012018

Cover Photo: Mike Egerton/Press Association/PA Wire URN:34968705/AP Images
Interior Photos: Mark J. Terrill/AP Images, 4-5, 14-15; Kyodo/AP Images, 6, 22; Sean Kilpatrick/CP/AP Images, 7; Bob Martin/Sports Illustrated/AP Images, 8-9; Tim Rue/Corbis Sport/Getty Images, 10-11; Brian Bahr/Getty Images Sport/Getty Images, 12-13; Lionel Cironneau/AP Images, 16; Mark Duncan/AP Images, 17; Chris Carlson/AP Images, 18-19; Andrew Milligan/Press Association/PA Wire URN:18970881/AP Images, 20-21; Kazuki Wakasugi/The Yomiuri Shimbun/AP Images, 23; Gregory Bull/AP Images, 24, 25; Scott Legato/Getty Images Entertainment/Getty Images, 26-27; Bret Hartman/AP Images, 28-29

Editor: Patrick Donnelly
Series Designer: Jake Nordby

Library of Congress Control Number: 2018936266

Publisher's Cataloging-in-Publication Data

Names: Hewson, Anthony K., author.
Title: Shaun White / by Anthony K. Hewson.
Description: Minneapolis, Minnesota : Abdo Publishing, 2019. | Series: Olympic Stars Set 2
    | Includes online resources and index.
Identifiers: ISBN 9781532116094 (lib.bdg.) | ISBN 9781532157073 (ebook)
Subjects: LCSH: White, Shaun, 1986---Juvenile literature. | Olympic athletes--Juvenile
    literature. | Winter Olympics--Juvenile literature. | Snowboarders--Juvenile
    literature. | Medalists--Juvenile literature.
Classification: DDC 796.93092 [B]--dc23

CONTENTS

THE TOMAHAWK 4

FROM SKATE TO SNOW 10

THE FLYING TOMATO 14

WHITE'S IMPACT 24

TIMELINE 30
GLOSSARY 31
INDEX 32
ABOUT THE AUTHOR 32

THE TOMAHAWK

Everyone was waiting to see what Shaun White would do. He was the most famous snowboarder in the world and the defending Olympic champion in the halfpipe. Now, at the 2010 Winter Games in Vancouver, British Columbia, White had already clinched another gold medal. None of the competitors had surpassed his score of 46.8 out of 50 on his first run.

But White knew he could do better. His last run was basically a victory lap. As he stood at the top of the halfpipe, he decided it was time to break out a new trick. He had been working on it in secret: the Double McTwist 1260. White called it "The Tomahawk."

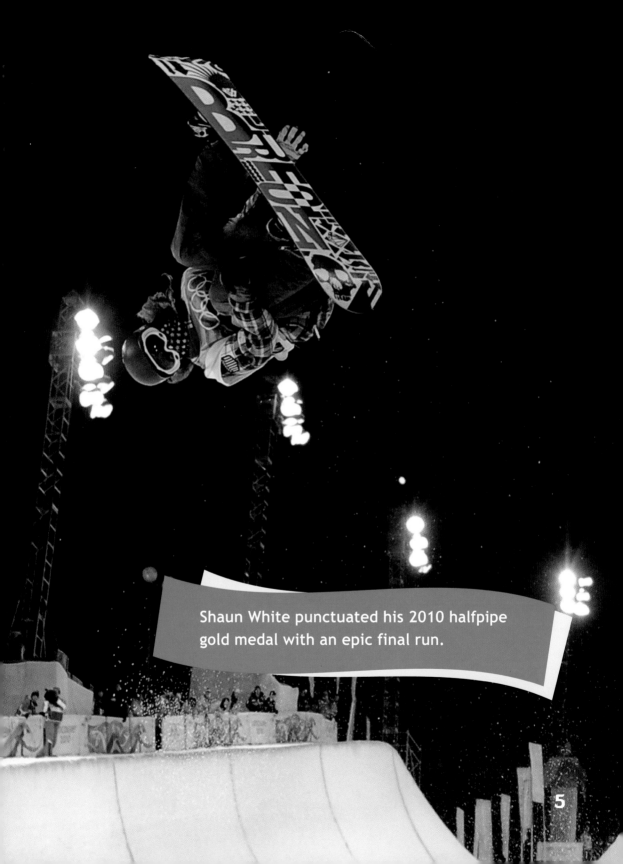

Shaun White punctuated his 2010 halfpipe gold medal with an epic final run.

Time-lapse
photography
showcases the
spins and flips of
White's tricks.

The Tomahawk consists of three and a half spins and two flips. White asked his coaches if he should do it. They encouraged him to try, but only if he could land it.

Not only was the trick difficult, it was dangerous. White hit his head practicing it at the X Games. But he kept working on it. He knew that if he perfected it, he could win any competition.

White flies high on his final run in Vancouver.

FAST FACT
Few other snowboarders posed a challenge to White in 2010. Silver medalist Peetu Piiroinen of Finland was the only other rider to score 45 or higher in the final round.

White took off down the pipe. His first few tricks were the same as his first run. He saved the Tomahawk for last. He got big air, flipping and spinning into the night sky.

The landing was clean, and White threw his arms into the air. He had just won his second Olympic gold medal. More important, he had changed snowboarding forever.

White celebrates bringing home another gold medal for Team USA.

Tony Hawk, *left*, mentored Shaun in the skateboarding world.

FROM SKATE
TO SNOW

Shaun White was born September 3, 1986, in San Diego, California. He grew up there, too. There isn't much snow in Southern California. Shaun's first love was skateboarding.

He was pretty good at it, too. By the time he was 7, even fellow San Diego skater Tony Hawk had noticed him at a skate park. But Shaun's brother Jesse had taken up snowboarding, and Shaun wanted to be just like him. The family started making the three-hour drive to the mountains for them to practice.

Shaun's skateboarding skills helped him quickly take to snowboarding. He started winning competitions. By age 13, companies were lining up to sponsor Shaun. He made his X Games debut that same year. He finished in 15th place, but the next year he broke into the top 10. And by 2003, Shaun had won his first X Games gold medal.

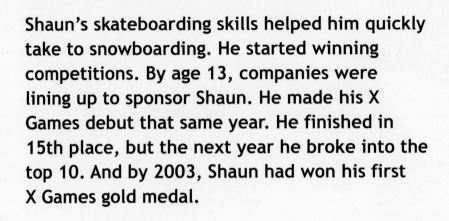

FAST FACT
Shaun White was born with a rare heart condition called tetralogy of Fallot. He had to have three heart surgeries as a young child to correct the problem.

Shaun participates in the US Snowboard Grand Prix in Breckenridge, Colorado, in January 2002.

THE FLYING TOMATO

When Shaun White was a kid, his fellow snowboarders called him "Future Boy." He had so much potential that everyone expected him to do incredible things.

By the time he was 18, the future had arrived. White won Winter X Games gold in 2003, 2004, 2005, and 2006. In 2003 and 2006 he won gold in both slopestyle and superpipe. But he became most famous for his abilities on the pipe.

White practices his other favorite sport at the 2006 Summer X Games.

White holds his fist in the air after his final halfpipe run at the 2006 Winter Games.

White was the favorite in halfpipe going into the 2006 Winter Olympics in Turin, Italy. But he was a bit shaky in his Olympic debut. After a stumble on his first run, White was in seventh place. He admitted to being nervous on the Olympic stage. But he rebounded to post the highest score in the second round to make the finals.

On his first run in the finals, White posted the highest score in Olympic halfpipe history. He nailed back-to-back 1080s and back-to-back 900s for a score of 46.8. That locked up his first Olympic gold medal.

American silver medalist Daniel Kass, *left*, and White celebrate their halfpipe success in Turin.

White won big at the 2010 ESPY Awards. His Olympic snowboarding achievements helped make him one of the most famous celebrities in the world.

With his curly red hair flying through the sky, White had a new nickname. He became known as "The Flying Tomato." He also was known as the best snowboarder in the world.

White continued to dominate the X Games, winning gold every year from 2008 to 2013. Red Bull, one of his sponsors, built him his own halfpipe in Colorado so he could practice for the 2010 Olympics. Rather than train where other snowboarders could see him, White could practice his new tricks in secret.

White's disappointing results in Sochi kept him off the medal podium for the first time at the Olympics.

White's historic trick at the Vancouver Games in 2010 kept him at the top of the snowboarding world. At the 2014 Olympics in Sochi, Russia, he was going for a third gold medal. White originally planned to compete in slopestyle as well. But he pulled out of that event just before the Games began.

Time spent training for slopestyle, plus working with a new coach, was distracting. White stumbled in the halfpipe and came home from an Olympics empty-handed for the first time. He called it the low point of his career. White dedicated himself to a comeback in 2018.

But disaster struck five months before the 2018 Games. White crashed while training at a World Cup event. He was trying a difficult cab double cork 1440. He ended up in the hospital with bruised lungs and cuts all over his face. He needed 62 stitches. But he recovered quickly, even posting a perfect score of 100 at a World Cup event in January.

By February, White was again the Olympic favorite. In PyeongChang, South Korea, he posted a 97.75 to win a record third gold medal. He did it with stitches still in his tongue from the crash.

White meets with reporters before his amazing performance in PyeongChang.

White recovered from his injury in time to compete at the Snowboard World Cup at Copper Mountain, Colorado, in December 2017.

FAST FACT

Team USA won gold in both men's and women's halfpipe at the 2018 Olympic Winter Games. Chloe Kim won the women's title. She has also landed a perfect 100 in her career.

White continues to test his athletic limits after nearly 20 years as a professional competitor.

WHITE'S IMPACT

Shaun White's three Olympic gold medals, numerous X Games medals, and incredible tricks make him the greatest snowboarder of all time. White continues to push the limits of what snowboarders can do. His gold-medal-winning run in 2006 included two 1080s. In 2018, he threw down back-to-back 1440s. That is one more complete 360-degree spin.

White has led the innovation of the sport of snowboarding. While his competitors were trying to land 1080s in 2010, White was mastering the 1260. He's always one spin ahead of the competition.

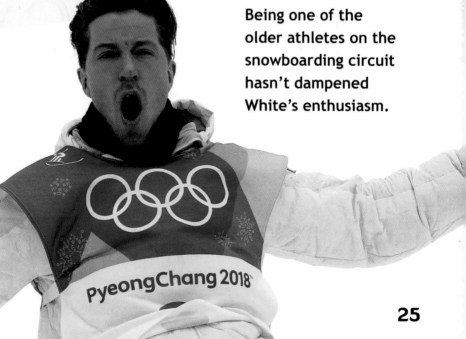

Being one of the older athletes on the snowboarding circuit hasn't dampened White's enthusiasm.

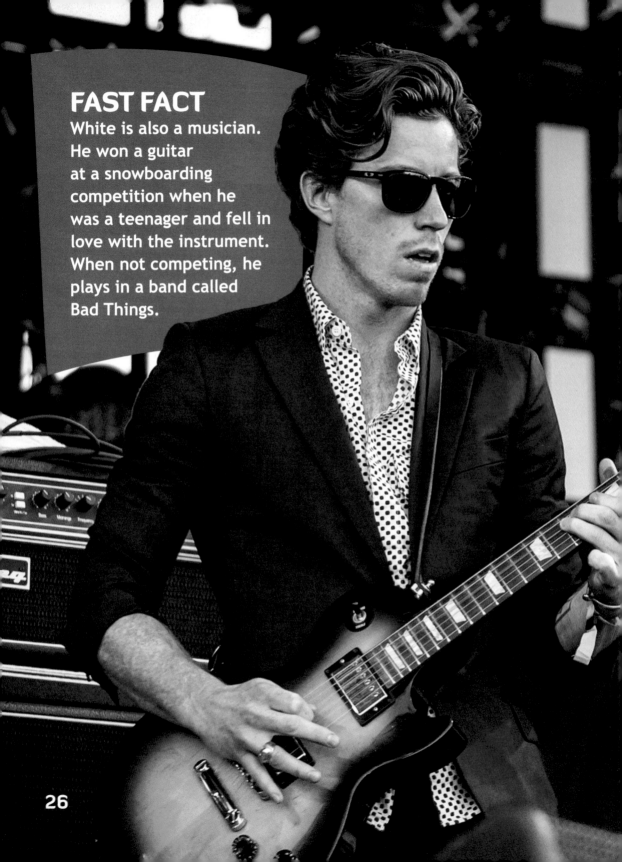

FAST FACT
White is also a musician. He won a guitar at a snowboarding competition when he was a teenager and fell in love with the instrument. When not competing, he plays in a band called Bad Things.

White, *left*, shows off his guitar skills with his bandmates.

Even at age 31 in 2018, White was still among the best in the world. Instead of inventing new moves, he worked on mastering the toughest tricks in the sport. He also showed no signs of slowing down. After PyeongChang, White left the door open for another Olympic appearance at the Beijing Games in 2022. But in between, he also wanted to go back to his first love.

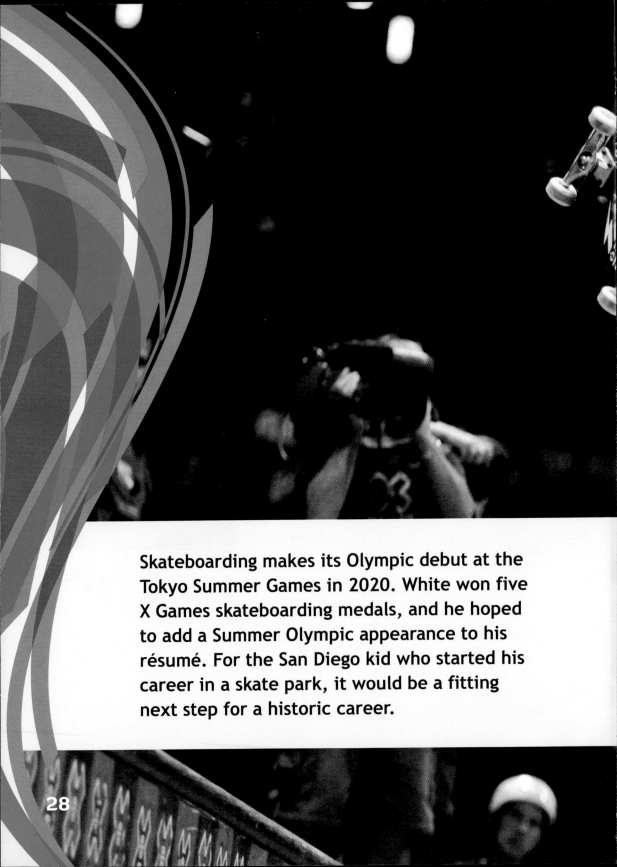

Skateboarding makes its Olympic debut at the Tokyo Summer Games in 2020. White won five X Games skateboarding medals, and he hoped to add a Summer Olympic appearance to his résumé. For the San Diego kid who started his career in a skate park, it would be a fitting next step for a historic career.

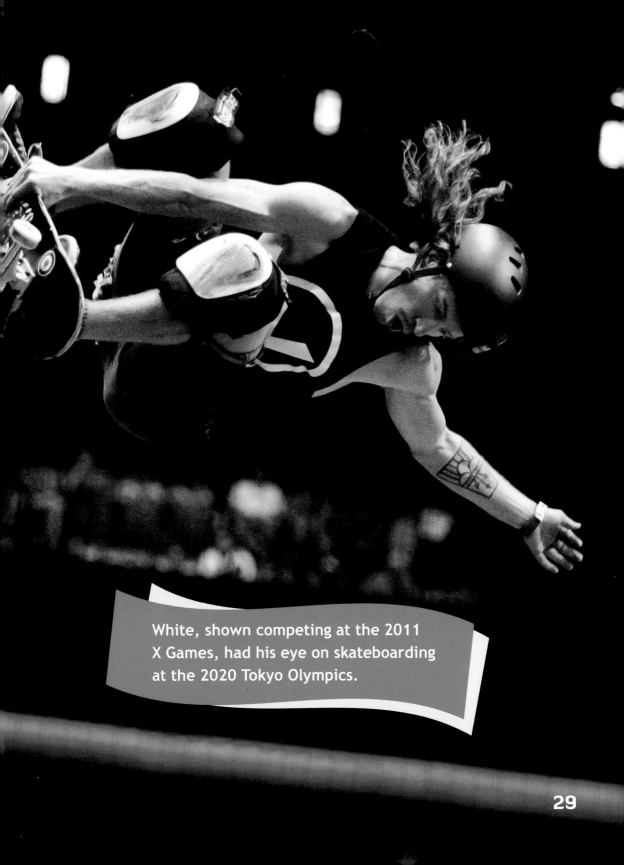

White, shown competing at the 2011
X Games, had his eye on skateboarding
at the 2020 Tokyo Olympics.

TIMELINE

1986

Shaun White is born on September 3 in San Diego, California.

2000

Shaun makes his X Games debut, finishing 15th in superpipe.

2002

Shaun wins his first X Games medals, silver in superpipe and slopestyle, one week after narrowly missing the US Olympic Team.

2003

Shaun breaks through with gold medals in superpipe and slopestyle at the X Games.

2006

With a record-high score, White wins his first Olympic gold medal at the Games in Turin, Italy.

2010

After securing his second Olympic gold medal, White lands his signature Tomahawk trick for the first time in competition.

2012

White becomes the first athlete to score a perfect 100 in superpipe at the X Games.

2014

For the first time, White fails to medal at an Olympic Games, finishing fourth in Sochi, Russia.

2018

In January, White lands another 100 at a World Cup event in Aspen, Colorado.

2018

White lands back-to-back 1440s for the first time in competition to earn his third Olympic gold medal in February in PyeongChang, South Korea.

GLOSSARY

clean
A snowboarding move that is performed perfectly.

debut
First appearance.

dominate
Remain at the top of a sport consistently over time.

favorite
The person or team expected to win a competition.

halfpipe
A venue for snowboarding and skiing consisting of a long, U-shaped ramp.

innovation
The process of coming up with new ways of doing something.

potential
Showing the ability to improve or develop in the future.

professional
Somebody who gets paid to perform an activity.

slopestyle
A snowboarding and skiing competition in which riders must perform tricks off ramps and pipes.

sponsor
A company that pays an athlete to promote or use its products.

victory lap
A run in which a snowboarder has already locked up the win, so he can attempt any tricks he wants.

INDEX

Bad Things, 26
Beijing, China, 27
Breckenridge,
   Colorado, 13

Copper Mountain,
   Colorado, 23

ESPY Awards, 18

Hawk, Tony, 10-11

Kass, Daniel, 17
Kim, Chloe, 23

Olympic Games, 4, 8,
   16-17, 19, 21-23, 25,
   27-29

Piiroinen, Peetu, 8
PyeongChang, South
   Korea, 22, 27

San Diego, California,
   11, 28
skateboarding, 10-12,
   15, 28, 29
Snowboard World Cup,
   23
Sochi, Russia, 21

tetralogy of Fallot, 12
Tokyo, Japan, 28-29
Turin, Italy, 17

US Snowboarding
   Grand Prix, 13

Vancouver, British
   Columbia, 4, 7, 21

White, Jesse, 11

X Games, 7, 12,
   14-15, 19, 25, 28-29

About the Author

Anthony K. Hewson is a freelance writer originally from
San Diego, now living in the Bay Area with his wife and their
two dogs.